I0012238

Quick Start Guide to Large Language Models (LLMs)

Contents

Introduction

Overview of LLMs

Large Language Models (LLMs) have revolutionized the field of artificial intelligence (AI) by enabling machines to understand and generate human-like text. These models, such as GPT-3 and BERT, are designed to process vast amounts of text data and generate contextually relevant responses. LLMs have found applications in various domains, from chatbots and virtual assistants to content creation and data analysis.

Importance and Applications

LLMs are critical in today's digital landscape due to their ability to perform complex language tasks with high accuracy. They are used in:

- **Customer Service**: Automating responses to customer inquiries.

- **Content Creation**: Generating articles, blogs, and social media posts.

- **Data Analysis**: Summarizing and interpreting large datasets.

- **Education**: Assisting with tutoring and providing personalized learning experiences.

- **Healthcare**: Supporting diagnostic tools and patient interactions.

Their versatility makes them indispensable across industries, improving efficiency and enabling new capabilities.

How to Use This Guide

This guide is designed to help you quickly understand and start working with LLMs. Each section builds on the previous one, guiding you from the basics to more advanced topics. Whether you're a beginner or an experienced practitioner, this guide provides practical insights and hands-on examples to help you harness the power of LLMs.

Getting Started

Prerequisites

Before diving into LLMs, ensure you have the following prerequisites:

- Basic understanding of programming, preferably in Python.

- Familiarity with machine learning concepts.

- A computer with internet access and sufficient computational resources.

Setting Up Your Environment

Setting up a proper environment is crucial for working with LLMs efficiently. Follow these steps:

1. **Choose an IDE**: Popular choices include Jupyter Notebook, PyCharm, or Visual Studio Code.

2. **Install Python**: Ensure you have Python 3.6 or later installed.

3. **Set Up a Virtual Environment**: Use venv or conda to create an isolated environment for your projects.

bash

Copy code

```
python -m venv llm_env
source llm_env/bin/activate          # On Windows, use `llm_env\Scripts\activate`
```

Installing Necessary Tools and Libraries

Install essential libraries and tools to get started with LLMs:

- **PyTorch**: A popular machine learning library.

  bash

  Copy code

  pip install torch

- **Transformers**: Hugging Face's library for working with LLMs.

  bash

  Copy code

  pip install transformers

- **Other Dependencies**: Depending on your project, you might need additional libraries like numpy, pandas, and scikit-learn.

bash

Copy code

pip install numpy pandas scikit-learn

Understanding LLMs

What Are LLMs?

Large Language Models are deep learning models trained on vast amounts of text data to understand, generate, and manipulate natural language. They leverage architectures like Transformers, which enable them to process text in parallel, making them highly efficient and effective.

Key Concepts and Terminology

- **Transformer**: An architecture that uses self-attention mechanisms to process text data.

- **Self-Attention**: A mechanism that allows the model to weigh the importance of different words in a sentence when making predictions.

- **Fine-Tuning**: The process of taking a pre-trained model and adapting it to a specific task or dataset.

- **Tokenization**: Breaking down text into smaller units (tokens) that the model can process.

Popular LLM Architectures

Several LLM architectures have gained prominence:

- **GPT (Generative Pre-trained Transformer)**: Developed by OpenAI, known for generating coherent and contextually relevant text.

- **BERT (Bidirectional Encoder Representations from Transformers)**: Developed by Google, excels in understanding the context of words in a sentence.

- **T5 (Text-to-Text Transfer Transformer)**: Converts all NLP tasks into a text-to-text format, making it highly versatile.

These architectures form the foundation of modern NLP applications, enabling breakthroughs in various language tasks.

Training Your First LLM

Data Collection and Preparation

The foundation of any successful LLM lies in the quality and quantity of data used for training. Here's how to approach data collection and preparation:

1. **Identify Data Sources**: Determine where your data will come from. This could include publicly available datasets, web scraping, or proprietary data sources.

2. **Data Cleaning**: Clean the collected data by removing duplicates, correcting errors, and standardizing formats. Ensure that the data is relevant to the task at hand.

3. **Data Annotation**: If your task requires labeled data (e.g., sentiment analysis), ensure that the data is accurately annotated. Use tools like Labelbox or Prodigy for efficient annotation.

4. **Data Splitting**: Split your dataset into training, validation, and test sets. A common split is 80% for training, 10% for validation, and 10% for testing.

Choosing the Right Model

Selecting the right LLM depends on your specific needs and the resources available. Consider the following factors:

1. **Task Requirements**: Identify the nature of your task. For text generation, GPT models are ideal, while BERT is better suited for text classification tasks.

2. **Model Size**: Larger models like GPT-3 offer better performance but require significant computational resources. Smaller models like DistilBERT provide a balance between performance and resource efficiency.

3. **Pre-trained Models**: Leverage pre-trained models available through libraries like Hugging Face's Transformers to save time and resources.

Training Process and Best Practices

Training an LLM involves several steps:

1. **Setting Up the Environment**: Ensure you have the necessary computational resources, such as GPUs or TPUs, and the required software libraries installed.

2. **Data Loading**: Use data loaders to efficiently feed data into your model during training.

3. **Model Configuration**: Configure your model with appropriate hyperparameters, such as learning rate, batch size, and number of training epochs.

4. **Training Loop**: Implement a training loop to iteratively update the model's weights. Monitor training metrics such as loss and accuracy to track progress.

5. **Validation**: Use the validation set to tune hyperparameters and avoid overfitting. Adjust settings based on validation performance.

6. **Checkpointing**: Save model checkpoints periodically to prevent data loss in case of interruptions.

Importance of Fine-Tuning

Fine-tuning allows you to adapt a pre-trained model to your specific task, improving performance and relevance. It requires less data and computational power compared to training a model from scratch.

Steps to Fine-Tune a Pretrained LLM

1. **Select a Pre-trained Model**: Choose a pre-trained model from a library like Hugging Face's Transformers.

2. **Prepare Your Data**: Ensure your dataset is formatted correctly and split into training and validation sets.

3. **Load the Model and Tokenizer**: Initialize the model and tokenizer with your chosen pre-trained model.

python

Copy code

```python
from transformers import AutoModelForSequenceClassification, AutoTokenizer


model_name = "bert-base-uncased"
```

```python
model = AutoModelForSequenceClassification.from_pretrained(model_name)
tokenizer = AutoTokenizer.from_pretrained(model_name)
```

4. **Tokenize Your Data**: Convert your text data into tokens that the model can process.

python

Copy code

```python
inputs = tokenizer(text, padding=True, truncation=True, return_tensors="pt")
```

5. **Set Up the Training Loop**: Define your training loop with appropriate loss functions and optimizers.

6. **Train the Model**: Run the training loop, periodically validating performance and adjusting hyperparameters as needed.

python

Copy code

```python
model.train()
for epoch in range(num_epochs):
```

```
for batch in train_dataloader:

    outputs = model(**batch)

    loss = outputs.loss

    loss.backward()

    optimizer.step()

    optimizer.zero_grad()
```

Practical Examples

For instance, fine-tuning BERT for sentiment analysis involves training it

on a dataset labeled with positive and negative sentiments. By adjusting the model's parameters to minimize the classification error on this specific task, you can achieve high accuracy in sentiment prediction.

Evaluation Metrics

- **Accuracy**: The proportion of correctly predicted samples.

- **Precision and Recall**: Measures of the relevance and completeness of the predictions.

- **F1 Score**: The harmonic mean of precision and recall, providing a balanced metric.

- **Perplexity**: Commonly used for language models, indicating how well the model predicts the next word in a sequence.

Tools and Techniques for Evaluation

- **Confusion Matrix**: Visual representation of the true vs. predicted labels.

- **ROC and AUC**: Receiver Operating Characteristic curve and Area Under the Curve for binary classification tasks.

- **Cross-Validation**: Splitting the data into multiple folds to validate the model on different subsets.

Interpreting Results

Analyze evaluation metrics to identify strengths and weaknesses in your model. For instance:

- **High Accuracy but Low Recall**: Indicates that the model is good at identifying positive samples but misses many true positives.
- **High Perplexity**: Suggests that the model struggles to predict the next word accurately, indicating the need for more data or a different model architecture.

Deploying LLMs

Deployment Options

Deploying Large Language Models (LLMs) effectively involves choosing the right deployment strategy based on your use case, scalability requirements, and infrastructure. Here are the primary options:

1. **Cloud-Based Deployment**: Utilize cloud services like AWS, Azure, or Google Cloud to host your LLMs. These platforms offer scalability, security, and various tools for managing AI workloads.

2. **On-Premises Deployment**: For organizations with strict data security requirements, deploying LLMs on local servers can provide greater control and compliance with data governance policies.

3. **Edge Deployment**: Deploying models on edge devices (e.g., smartphones, IoT devices) is useful for applications needing real-time processing with low latency.

4. **Containerization**: Using Docker containers to encapsulate your LLM and its dependencies ensures consistent deployment across different environments. Tools like Kubernetes can manage and scale containerized applications.

Integration with Applications

Integrating LLMs with existing applications involves several steps:

1. **API Development**: Create RESTful or GraphQL APIs to interact with your LLM. Frameworks like Flask or FastAPI can help you build robust APIs quickly.

2. **Frontend Integration**: Connect your APIs to frontend applications (web, mobile) using standard HTTP requests. Ensure seamless user interactions by handling responses efficiently.

3. **Middleware**: Use middleware to preprocess inputs and postprocess outputs. This includes tasks like tokenization, decoding, and error handling.

4. **Security**: Implement authentication and authorization mechanisms to protect your API endpoints. Use tools like OAuth2, JWT, and API gateways.

Monitoring and Maintenance

Maintaining a deployed LLM involves continuous monitoring and regular updates:

1. **Performance Monitoring**: Use monitoring tools like Prometheus, Grafana, or CloudWatch to track metrics such as latency, throughput, and error rates.

2. **Model Updates**: Regularly update your models with new data and retrain them to improve accuracy and relevance.

3. **Logging and Alerts**: Implement logging to capture detailed information about model predictions and set up alerts for any anomalies or performance drops.

4. **Scalability**: Ensure your deployment can scale horizontally by adding more instances or vertically by enhancing hardware resources.

Advanced Topics

Transfer Learning with LLMs

Transfer learning allows you to leverage pre-trained models and adapt them to specific tasks with limited data:

1. **Fine-Tuning**: Adjust the weights of a pre-trained model by training it on your specific dataset.

2. **Feature Extraction**: Use the pre-trained model as a feature extractor and train a simpler model on top of these features for your specific task.

3. **Domain Adaptation**: Adapt models to work better in specific domains (e.g., medical, legal) by fine-tuning on domain-specific data.

Handling Large Datasets

Efficiently managing large datasets is crucial for training and deploying LLMs:

1. **Data Storage**: Use distributed storage solutions like HDFS, Amazon S3, or Google Cloud Storage to store large datasets.

2. **Data Loading**: Employ data loading libraries such as TensorFlow Data or PyTorch's DataLoader to handle large datasets efficiently.

3. **Batch Processing**: Split data into manageable batches to ensure smooth training and inference processes.

Optimizing Performance

Optimizing LLM performance involves several techniques:

1. **Quantization**: Reduce model size and inference time by converting weights from floating-point to lower precision (e.g., int8).

2. **Distillation**: Create smaller, faster models by distilling knowledge from larger models.

3. **Parallelism**: Utilize model parallelism and data parallelism to distribute computation across multiple GPUs or TPUs.

Real-World Applications

Case Studies

- **Customer Support**: A leading e-commerce company deployed an LLM to automate customer service, reducing response times and operational costs while maintaining high customer satisfaction.
- **Content Generation**: A media company uses LLMs to generate news articles, enhancing productivity and allowing journalists to focus on investigative work.

Industry-Specific Use Cases

- **Healthcare**: LLMs assist in diagnosing diseases by analyzing patient data and medical literature.
- **Finance**: Financial institutions use LLMs for sentiment analysis, fraud detection, and automated report generation.
- **Education**: LLMs provide personalized tutoring and generate educational content tailored to individual learning styles.

- **Case Study 1: Enhancing Customer Support with Real-Time Language Models at Scale**

- A multinational telecom company sought to improve its customer support by reducing response times and improving customer satisfaction. With over 10,000 inquiries daily, manual handling was inefficient, costly, and error-prone. They implemented a real-time LLM-powered chatbot for customer interactions, allowing for automatic responses to common issues, account inquiries, and troubleshooting questions.

- The company chose an LLM fine-tuned specifically for customer support, using proprietary datasets from past interactions. They adopted few-shot learning to keep the model updated with recent changes in product offerings and policies without extensive retraining. To maintain context across interactions, the chatbot utilized in-context learning, allowing it to refer back to prior customer information within the session.

- In addition to common questions, the chatbot was trained to escalate complex issues to human agents, integrating smoothly with the existing support system. To improve its response quality, feedback loops were implemented where human agents rated the chatbot's responses, contributing to a growing dataset for continual improvement. Real-time monitoring ensured performance stability and allowed for adjustments when unusual query patterns emerged.

- The implementation reduced average response times by 60%, resulting in a 40% improvement in customer satisfaction scores. The chatbot also lowered operational costs by 30% by handling routine inquiries autonomously, freeing up agents for more complex cases. This scalable approach allowed the company to extend support hours without increasing staffing costs, demonstrating LLMs' capacity to transform high-demand support environments.

- **Case Study 2: Revolutionizing Legal Research with LLMs in a Law Firm**

- A top-tier law firm wanted to streamline legal research, a labor-intensive process requiring attorneys to review thousands of pages to find relevant precedents and legal interpretations. With LLM technology, the firm developed a specialized tool to parse legal documents, identify relevant case law, and provide contextually accurate summaries.

- To create a domain-specific LLM, the firm fine-tuned an open-source language model on a proprietary legal dataset, which included case documents, statutes, and legal annotations. In-context learning was used to support query-specific responses, where attorneys could input specific legal questions and receive customized, concise summaries. Advanced filtering algorithms were integrated to prioritize the most relevant cases based on recent citations and legal importance.

- One of the LLM's standout features was its semantic search capability, which allowed attorneys to search legal documents using natural language instead of precise keywords. The model's embeddings helped identify synonymous legal terms, making it easier to uncover relevant cases even if phrasing differed across documents.

- The LLM-powered tool cut research time by 50%, allowing attorneys to focus on analysis rather than document retrieval. The firm reported a 20% increase in productivity and a faster case turnaround. Furthermore, it enhanced case preparation quality, as attorneys had quicker access to more nuanced and recent case information, giving them an advantage in court.

- **Case Study 3: Personalized Learning in Education with Adaptive LLM Systems**
- A leading online education platform sought to personalize learning for students across diverse backgrounds and learning speeds. Their goal was to create an adaptive LLM-powered tutor that could adjust to each student's progress, reinforce concepts, and clarify doubts in real-time.
- The platform implemented a custom-trained LLM fine-tuned on a large educational dataset, which included textbooks, lectures, and problem-solving examples. Using few-shot learning, the model adapted to different subjects, providing context-aware responses across topics from mathematics to language arts. In addition, the LLM could generate custom quizzes and explanations based on each student's current performance.
- To make the tool more engaging, the company integrated interactive, in-context feedback mechanisms. The LLM dynamically adjusted content difficulty by assessing student responses and offering personalized hints. This allowed struggling students to

receive additional support, while advanced students were given more challenging tasks.

- The adaptive LLM improved student engagement rates by 25% and boosted learning outcomes by 30%. Students rated the experience highly, citing the tool's responsiveness and personalized approach. Teachers could also monitor real-time analytics, identifying students who needed extra support, which reduced dropout rates. This personalized, data-driven model highlighted how LLMs can scale individualized learning experiences, especially in remote and diverse educational settings.

- **Case Study 4: Enhancing Drug Discovery with Generative AI in Pharmaceutical Research**

- A pharmaceutical company aimed to accelerate drug discovery, a costly and time-consuming process. They adopted an LLM-based solution to analyze chemical data, propose novel compound structures, and predict interactions with biological targets, leveraging a custom generative model.

- To start, the company trained the LLM on chemical and biomedical datasets, including molecular structures and pharmacokinetic properties. Generative capabilities allowed the model to create new compound structures based on predefined therapeutic targets. Using embeddings, the model evaluated potential drug compounds by assessing chemical similarity and predicting efficacy.

- One critical feature was the model's ability to run virtual screening processes, which eliminated weak candidates early on, significantly reducing the number of compounds requiring laboratory testing. In addition, it incorporated real-time feedback on compounds' safety profiles, refining the candidate list to focus on the safest, most effective options.

- The LLM accelerated the drug discovery process, reducing compound screening time by 40% and cutting R&D costs by 35%. Within a year, the company identified several promising compounds for preclinical trials. The success underscored the potential of LLMs in not only accelerating innovation but also reducing costs in life sciences by identifying viable drug candidates more efficiently.

- **Case Study 5: Financial Fraud Detection with an LLM in Real-Time Banking Systems**

- A large bank faced rising financial fraud and sought to enhance fraud detection with real-time LLM-based analysis. The model needed to process vast amounts of transaction data, flagging suspicious patterns without affecting user experience or transaction speed.

- The bank trained the LLM on transaction datasets, using a combination of supervised and unsupervised learning. In-context learning allowed the model to understand specific fraud types, while embeddings captured transactional patterns like location, time, and transaction amount, helping identify anomalies across accounts.

- The LLM was integrated with the bank's fraud detection pipeline, where it continuously analyzed new transactions, scoring them for potential fraud. High-risk transactions were flagged for human review, while low-risk ones continued without interruption. Real-time monitoring provided additional control, ensuring that false positives were minimized to avoid customer inconvenience.

- The LLM's deployment reduced fraud cases by 45%, preventing significant financial losses. Its real-time processing allowed the bank to respond to potential threats almost instantly, improving

customer trust and security. Additionally, the solution provided a

scalable approach to fraud detection, adapting to emerging fraud

tactics through periodic retraining, thus keeping the model relevant

in an ever-evolving threat landscape.

- **Case Study 6: Interactive Customer Education for a Retail Pharmacy Chain**

- A retail pharmacy chain wanted to provide accessible, reliable information to customers regarding medications, supplements, and general health inquiries. Traditional customer support channels couldn't meet the demand for detailed guidance, so the chain developed an LLM-powered chatbot to serve as an educational resource.

- Trained on pharmaceutical databases, regulatory guidelines, and health FAQs, the LLM provided accurate, user-friendly answers to customers' health-related questions. Integrated into the pharmacy's mobile app, the LLM chatbot offered 24/7 support, guiding customers on proper usage, potential interactions, and lifestyle suggestions for common health issues.

- Customers valued the easy access to information, leading to a 30% increase in satisfaction and stronger brand loyalty. The pharmacy chain also benefited from reduced support costs, as fewer in-person consultations were required for routine questions. This case underscores how LLMs can effectively educate and empower consumers in healthcare, improving customer experience and

operational efficiency.

- **Case Study 7: Optimizing Supply Chain Operations with Demand Forecasting**

- A logistics company with a global supply chain faced challenges in accurately forecasting demand, leading to frequent stockouts and excess inventory. Traditional methods struggled to process the vast amount of data involved. By implementing an LLM trained on historical sales, seasonality, and external market factors, the company optimized its demand forecasting.

- The LLM generated precise predictions, adjusting for real-time factors like holidays, weather, and market trends. The model was also configured to highlight potential disruptions, such as changes in shipping routes or delays, allowing for proactive adjustments in inventory management.

- This solution reduced stockouts by 40% and cut excess inventory by 30%, leading to lower holding costs and improved customer satisfaction. The company achieved a more resilient supply chain, showcasing LLMs' capability to enhance logistics and operational decision-making.

-

- **Case Study 8: Advanced Fraud Detection in Financial Services**

- A leading bank wanted to improve its fraud detection capabilities in response to evolving cyber threats. Traditional rule-based systems couldn't keep up with increasingly sophisticated fraud tactics. The bank implemented an LLM to analyze transactions in real time and detect anomalies indicative of fraudulent activity.
- The model was trained on a vast dataset of normal and fraudulent transactions. Using embeddings to capture behavioral patterns, it flagged unusual activity, such as geographic discrepancies or atypical spending patterns, while maintaining a low false-positive rate.
- The LLM-enabled system reduced fraud losses by 45%, enabling the bank to respond to threats almost instantly. Customers appreciated the enhanced security, leading to improved trust and loyalty. This case demonstrates how LLMs can provide advanced, real-time analysis for financial security, safeguarding both institutions and customers.
-
- **Case Study 9: Accelerating Drug Discovery in Pharmaceutical Research**

- A pharmaceutical company sought to accelerate its drug discovery process, a traditionally slow and expensive endeavor. They deployed an LLM to analyze chemical structures and predict interactions with biological targets, aiming to identify promising compounds faster.

- The model was trained on biomedical research, molecular data, and prior drug trials. It generated potential compounds based on predefined therapeutic goals, scoring each for effectiveness and safety. The LLM's predictions helped narrow down viable candidates, which were then prioritized for lab testing.

- This LLM-powered approach reduced research time by 40%, leading to faster drug candidate identification and reduced R&D costs. By accelerating drug discovery, the pharmaceutical company gained a significant advantage in bringing new treatments to market, highlighting the transformative impact of AI on life sciences.

-
- **Case Study 10: Enhancing Customer Support for a Telecommunications Provider**

- A major telecommunications provider struggled to handle a high volume of customer inquiries. Simple questions, such as billing or troubleshooting, took up substantial support time, reducing efficiency and customer satisfaction. To address this, the company implemented an LLM-driven virtual assistant capable of handling basic inquiries.

- Trained on past support logs, common troubleshooting steps, and FAQs, the LLM could assist customers 24/7, offering solutions without requiring human intervention for simple issues. Additionally, the assistant escalated complex queries to human agents, streamlining the workflow and enabling faster response times.

- This resulted in a 60% reduction in wait times for customers, with support satisfaction scores rising by 35%. The provider also saved on operational costs, as fewer agents were required for routine inquiries. This case exemplifies how LLMs can deliver enhanced customer support and improve operational efficiency in high-demand environments.

- **Case Study 11: Automating Compliance Checks in Insurance**

- An insurance company faced strict regulatory requirements, leading to extensive time and resources spent on compliance checks. The company introduced an LLM to review policies, claims, and documentation for adherence to industry standards and regulations.

- The LLM was trained on regulatory guidelines, historical compliance cases, and claims data. By analyzing documents, the model flagged potential compliance issues and provided reasons for its recommendations. This enabled compliance officers to review flagged cases more efficiently, focusing on higher-risk areas.

- With this solution, compliance review times were cut by 50%, and the company achieved a 30% reduction in compliance-related penalties. This case demonstrates how LLMs can streamline regulatory tasks, reducing manual workloads and helping businesses stay compliant with industry standards.

- **Case Study 12: Personalized Virtual Tutoring for Education Platforms**

- An online education platform wanted to offer personalized support to students, but the demand outpaced the availability of live tutors. The platform deployed an LLM as a virtual tutor, capable of answering questions and explaining complex topics in real time.

- The LLM was fine-tuned with course content, including textbooks, practice exams, and study guides. It used natural language processing to understand students' questions and provide tailored responses, adapting its explanations based on student feedback to improve over time.

- Students reported higher engagement and improved understanding, with the platform seeing a 25% increase in retention rates. Additionally, the LLM tutor allowed the platform to expand without needing additional human tutors. This case illustrates how LLMs can offer scalable, individualized support, enhancing the learning experience for students.

-

- **Case Study 13: Boosting Product Recommendations in E-Commerce**

- An online retailer sought to improve product recommendations, as existing algorithms didn't capture individual preferences effectively. The company introduced an LLM trained on customer reviews, purchase histories, and browsing data to deliver highly personalized recommendations.

- The LLM could identify patterns in user behavior and adapt suggestions based on real-time factors, such as seasonality and trending items. This helped the retailer offer more relevant product recommendations, increasing conversion rates and customer satisfaction.

- The implementation resulted in a 35% increase in sales from recommended products and a noticeable improvement in customer engagement. This case shows how LLMs can create richer, more intuitive recommendation systems that adapt to customer needs.

- **Case Study 14: Legal Document Review for Law Firms**

- A law firm faced the challenge of processing extensive documentation for cases, which involved manually reviewing contracts, discovery documents, and case files. The firm adopted an LLM to assist in document review, allowing lawyers to focus on higher-value tasks.

- Trained on legal documents, case precedents, and statutory language, the LLM quickly highlighted relevant sections and summarized complex legal jargon. It flagged potential issues or clauses requiring closer scrutiny, making the review process significantly more efficient.

- This resulted in a 40% reduction in time spent on document review, enabling lawyers to take on more cases and improve client service. This case highlights the role of LLMs in the legal industry, where they can streamline labor-intensive tasks and enhance productivity.

- **Case Study 15: Sentiment Analysis for Social Media Marketing**

- A fashion brand wanted to understand customer sentiment toward its products and campaigns. The company deployed an LLM to analyze social media mentions, reviews, and customer feedback, gaining insights into brand perception.

- The LLM was trained on various social media platforms to interpret the nuances of slang, emojis, and informal language often used by customers. It categorized feedback by sentiment, identifying areas of positive feedback and areas needing improvement.
- The brand used these insights to adjust its campaigns, resulting in a 20% increase in positive sentiment and engagement across social channels. This case showcases how LLMs can provide brands with a deeper understanding of customer perceptions, allowing for more responsive and targeted marketing.

Future Trends

- **Multimodal Models**: Combining text, image, and audio inputs for richer and more accurate predictions.

- **Smaller, More Efficient Models**: Development of compact models that retain the capabilities of larger LLMs but are more resource-efficient.

- **Ethical AI**: Increasing focus on developing LLMs that are fair, transparent, and accountable.

Common Challenges and Solutions

Debugging Tips

- **Log Details**: Implement extensive logging to capture detailed information about model inputs, outputs, and intermediate steps.

- **Interactive Debugging**: Use interactive tools like Jupyter notebooks or Colab to test and debug code snippets in isolation.

Performance Issues

- **Bottleneck Identification**: Use profiling tools to identify and address performance bottlenecks in your code or hardware setup.

- **Resource Allocation**: Ensure optimal allocation of computational resources by balancing workloads across CPUs, GPUs, and TPUs.
- **Advanced Training Techniques for LLMs**
- Training LLMs is a complex process that requires a blend of machine learning techniques, data engineering, and deep learning skills. Advanced training techniques can drastically improve the model's performance, robustness, and applicability in specific domains. This chapter covers distributed training, large-scale data handling, and strategies for efficient learning while reducing computational costs.
- Distributed training techniques like model parallelism and data parallelism are key in scaling up training on large datasets and across multiple nodes. With model parallelism, we split the LLM across multiple devices, managing memory constraints and training speed. Conversely, data parallelism distributes the data across nodes but keeps the model intact across devices, making it easier to train using gradient descent.
- In addition, data optimization through augmentation and synthetic generation can improve training outcomes. Data augmentation helps with data diversity and avoids overfitting, a common issue in

LLMs. By generating synthetic data, we can expand the dataset with less cost, particularly useful in niche applications like medical and legal text.

- Another critical aspect is efficient learning strategies such as transfer learning and curriculum learning. Transfer learning allows you to leverage pre-trained models on large datasets, reducing the amount of data needed for domain-specific training. Curriculum learning, where the model is trained in stages with increasing difficulty, can enhance its comprehension and generalization abilities. To balance these techniques, a mix of curriculum learning followed by transfer learning can help develop models with strong generalization capabilities in less time.

- Lastly, adaptive learning rates and gradient clipping are crucial in LLM training. Gradient clipping mitigates exploding gradients by limiting their size, which keeps the training process stable. Adaptive learning rates help optimize performance by adjusting according to model progress, preventing overshooting or vanishing gradients.

In-Context Learning and Few-Shot Techniques

In-context learning (ICL) and few-shot techniques represent a paradigm

shift for how LLMs handle contextual information. Instead of retraining the model, we provide examples directly within the prompt, which the model then uses to infer patterns. This approach saves time and resources, making it an efficient technique for real-time applications.

Few-shot learning provides the model with a handful of examples, enabling it to perform new tasks with minimal data. This method is advantageous in applications where extensive data is either unavailable or too costly to acquire. By observing just a few examples, the model adjusts its response, which is invaluable in applications like dynamic chatbots, personalized recommendations, or summarization tasks where input varies widely.

Zero-shot learning takes this a step further by requiring no examples at all. It leverages the model's general knowledge from pre-training, making it versatile in general-purpose applications. When combined with few-shot techniques, zero-shot applications can make LLMs highly adaptable, allowing them to generalize well across tasks with little to no additional information.

Moreover, ICL and few-shot techniques benefit greatly from embeddings, which capture semantic information across contexts. By creating custom embeddings for specific use cases, the model can interpret nuanced queries more effectively. A well-implemented embedding strategy allows LLMs to manage complex contextual relationships and even domain-specific language, like legal or medical terminology.

An advanced application of ICL and few-shot techniques includes developing modular responses in interactive systems, where context continuously shifts. For example, in a customer service bot, using ICL enables the model to maintain context across conversations, tailoring its responses based on previously gathered information. This application reduces response times and improves accuracy, essential for high-stakes environments.

Ethical and Bias Mitigation Strategies for LLMs

As LLMs become integrated into various domains, mitigating bias and ethical concerns is increasingly important. Addressing bias involves a proactive approach in both data selection and model training phases to ensure inclusivity and fairness across all user interactions. Ethical guidelines and regular audits during model development are essential for maintaining transparent and accountable AI.

One of the most effective methods of bias mitigation is adversarial training, where models are trained with both biased and unbiased data to differentiate and discard biased patterns. This approach requires a carefully curated dataset and often involves input from subject matter experts to identify and label potential bias indicators.

Additionally, differential privacy mechanisms, which add noise to the data, help in preserving user privacy and mitigating bias in data collection. Another method, known as federated learning, decentralizes training by allowing the model to learn across devices without transferring raw data. These techniques ensure privacy and mitigate the risks associated with centralized data, often vulnerable to bias from data originating from limited sources.

Explainability in LLMs is equally vital for understanding potential biases. By implementing interpretable models and creating transparent layers in the model architecture, developers can analyze and understand why certain responses are generated. Techniques like Local Interpretable Model-Agnostic Explanations (LIME) and SHapley Additive exPlanations (SHAP) help in revealing decision-making patterns in opaque models.

Ethical AI frameworks recommend frequent model retraining and cross-audits to spot and address bias that may arise over time. Regular audits and real-time monitoring help ensure that bias mitigation is a continuous process rather than a one-time solution. These audits should include stakeholders from diverse backgrounds, encompassing legal, social, and technical expertise to provide a well-rounded perspective on fairness and accountability.

Real-Time Model Monitoring and Maintenance

Real-time monitoring and maintenance are essential for keeping LLMs operational and accurate over time. Post-deployment, models can encounter data drift or evolving contexts, necessitating ongoing evaluation and adaptation. Monitoring involves tracking key metrics such as accuracy, latency, and user satisfaction to assess model health and effectiveness.

One popular method for real-time monitoring is setting up an anomaly detection system to catch unexpected changes in model output. This setup helps in identifying and addressing drift or out-of-distribution data in real-time. Anomaly detection can trigger retraining or fine-tuning processes when necessary, keeping the model up-to-date and aligned with evolving user needs.

To ensure stability, monitoring pipelines should be built with automatic failover and fallback strategies. For instance, if the LLM begins to exhibit unexpected behaviors, the system can revert to a simpler model or predefined response templates until issues are resolved. This approach minimizes downtime and mitigates the impact on end-users.

Implementing observability dashboards provides a centralized view of model metrics, making it easier for teams to monitor performance. Integrating these dashboards with real-time logging tools allows for rapid debugging and optimization. The use of specialized metrics, such as perplexity and semantic similarity, provides insights into the model's linguistic coherence and content relevance over time.

In addition to monitoring, maintenance encompasses regular updates, bug fixes, and retraining cycles. Scheduled retraining, based on accumulated data, enables the model to adapt to long-term changes in data patterns. In dynamic environments like social media or finance, frequent model updates are critical for maintaining relevancy and accuracy in predictions and recommendations.

Advanced Model Compression and Optimization Techniques

As LLMs continue to grow in size, optimizing them for speed and efficiency becomes a priority, particularly for deployment on devices with limited resources. Model compression techniques, including pruning, quantization, and distillation, are fundamental to deploying LLMs in resource-constrained settings without sacrificing performance.

Model pruning involves removing redundant or low-impact neurons, effectively reducing the model's size and computational demand. Structured pruning, which targets specific layers or blocks, ensures that the model architecture remains coherent, leading to efficient and predictable reductions in size.

Quantization converts weights and activations from floating-point precision to lower bit widths, like 8-bit integers, making the model faster while preserving accuracy. Quantization-aware training further enhances performance by training the model to anticipate lower precision. This technique is widely used in edge deployments and real-time applications where speed is critical.

Model distillation is another effective strategy, where a smaller "student" model learns from a large, pre-trained "teacher" model. This process preserves the knowledge captured by the teacher model, often yielding a student model that performs comparably but requires far fewer resources. Distillation can also involve selective training to preserve specific skills, making the student model ideal for niche applications.

Another optimization technique, known as neural architecture search (NAS), automatically searches for and fine-tunes architectures optimized for specific tasks. This approach uses algorithms to create and test multiple architectures, selecting the one that balances speed and accuracy. NAS, combined with techniques like early stopping and dynamic batching, can significantly reduce computational demands and costs in LLM deployment.

Chapter: Optimizing Model Efficiency with Knowledge Distillation and Quantization

In the realm of large language models, efficiency is key to deploying models effectively, especially in real-world applications where computational resources may be limited. Knowledge distillation and quantization are two powerful techniques that can make LLMs more practical and efficient while maintaining high performance.

Knowledge Distillation for Model Compression

Knowledge distillation is a model compression technique that allows us to transfer the knowledge of a large, complex model (known as the "teacher" model) to a smaller, simpler model (the "student" model). By imitating the predictions and generalization patterns of the teacher, the student model achieves similar performance with fewer parameters, making it faster and less memory-intensive.

To implement knowledge distillation effectively in an LLM, the teacher model's output probabilities over potential tokens in each step are used to "teach" the student. During training, the student learns to mimic the behavior of the teacher. This is achieved by adjusting the loss function to emphasize alignment with the teacher's predictions rather than solely aiming for accuracy in matching training labels.

The benefits are clear: reducing the model size can make it feasible to deploy on less powerful hardware, including mobile devices and edge computing setups. Additionally, a distilled model can often perform inference faster, which is crucial for applications requiring low latency.

Quantization for Model Compression

Quantization is another strategy to reduce model size and enhance computational efficiency. Quantization techniques involve representing model weights and activations with fewer bits than the typical 32-bit floating-point numbers. For instance, 8-bit integer quantization can greatly reduce the model size, leading to faster computation without significantly sacrificing accuracy.

Quantization works well with LLMs by minimizing the computational footprint. Using techniques such as dynamic or static quantization allows portions of the model to be quantized selectively, so that only the less accuracy-sensitive components are affected. This approach can yield significant reductions in model size and speed up inference times, especially when applied to hardware designed to accelerate lower-precision operations, such as TPUs.

These methods help to make LLMs more accessible for a wide range of applications, from real-time translation on mobile devices to deployment in cost-constrained cloud environments.

Chapter: Advanced Fine-Tuning Techniques for Domain-Specific Applications

Fine-tuning is critical for adapting general-purpose language models to specific industries and use cases. However, fine-tuning for advanced applications often requires specialized techniques to achieve optimal performance, especially when working with limited labeled data or highly domain-specific information.

Domain-Adaptive Pretraining (DAPT)

Domain-adaptive pretraining is a technique where a general-purpose LLM is pretrained on a corpus specific to the desired domain before fine-tuning. This approach helps the model learn patterns and terminologies prevalent in a given field, such as legal, medical, or financial domains.

For instance, a model adapted to the medical domain would be pretrained on large collections of medical literature, research papers, and clinical trial data. This adaptation allows the model to grasp the unique linguistic patterns and domain knowledge needed for high-quality results in downstream tasks, such as diagnosing patient symptoms or summarizing clinical reports.

Data Augmentation for Low-Resource Fine-Tuning

When labeled data is scarce, data augmentation can create synthetic training examples, which expands the training dataset and improves model generalization. Techniques such as synonym replacement, paraphrasing, and back-translation help in generating variations of existing text, enriching the dataset without requiring additional manual labeling.

Additionally, the use of large-scale unsupervised corpora can support self-supervised learning, which is another way of enhancing the LLM's capability without the need for manual labeling. These methods improve the model's understanding of nuances and variations in language, which is especially useful for industry-specific vocabulary and structure.

Multi-Task Learning (MTL) for Enhanced Versatility

Multi-task learning involves fine-tuning the model to handle multiple related tasks simultaneously, which enhances versatility. For example, a legal-focused LLM could be trained to perform tasks like contract summarization, legal question answering, and clause extraction within a single training cycle. MTL helps the model learn to generalize better across related tasks, which can improve performance on each individual task by leveraging shared knowledge.

These advanced fine-tuning techniques enable LLMs to perform exceptionally well in specialized applications, allowing organizations to derive more accurate and contextually relevant insights from their models.

Chapter: Implementing Federated Learning for Privacy-Conscious LLM Training

Federated learning is a technique that allows models to be trained across multiple devices or servers without transferring the raw data to a central location. This approach has gained significant traction in privacy-sensitive domains like healthcare and finance, where data confidentiality is paramount.

Federated Learning Workflow for LLMs

In federated learning, an LLM can be trained by distributing the training process across multiple devices (clients). Each client trains a local model on its own data, and the local models are then sent to a central server, which aggregates the updates to create a global model. The global model is then distributed back to the clients for further training.

This approach ensures that sensitive data remains on the client devices, thus minimizing privacy risks. The LLM benefits from the diversity of data across clients while keeping the raw data decentralized and private. Federated learning can also reduce latency by keeping the training local and enabling models to adapt to real-time changes in user behavior.

Model Aggregation and Secure Computation

Aggregating models in federated learning can be challenging, as it requires a way to update the global model without compromising individual client data. Techniques like secure aggregation and differential privacy ensure that client data is anonymized and protected from any potential leaks. Secure aggregation techniques compute updates in a way that keeps individual updates confidential, allowing the server to update the global model without seeing each client's data.

Overcoming Federated Learning Challenges

Implementing federated learning for LLMs introduces unique challenges, such as handling variable data quality and uneven participation rates among clients. To mitigate these, techniques like adaptive learning rates and periodic rebalancing of client contributions can help stabilize the learning process.

By using federated learning, organizations can create LLMs that respect data privacy regulations, making this approach ideal for sectors with strict data protection requirements. It opens the door for privacy-preserving AI in various applications, from mobile devices to healthcare diagnostics, enabling organizations to build responsible AI solutions that protect user

data.

Chapter: Distributed Training Techniques for Large-Scale LLMs

As LLMs continue to grow in size and complexity, training them requires significant computational resources, which is often beyond the capability of a single machine. Distributed training techniques are essential for scaling LLM training across multiple GPUs, TPUs, or nodes in a cluster. This chapter delves into strategies and technologies that enable efficient large-scale training of LLMs.

Data Parallelism vs. Model Parallelism

When implementing distributed training, one of the fundamental decisions is whether to use data parallelism, model parallelism, or a hybrid of both.

- **Data Parallelism**: In data parallelism, multiple copies of the model are deployed across different GPUs or nodes, with each processing a unique batch of data. The gradients from each copy are aggregated and averaged to update the global model. This approach is effective for models that fit within a single GPU's memory but need multiple GPUs for faster processing.

- **Model Parallelism**: Model parallelism is required when the model is too large to fit in a single GPU's memory. This approach splits the model across multiple GPUs, allowing each device to handle a portion of the model. Each GPU processes a segment of the input sequentially, with the data passing through various parts of the model hosted across GPUs. Although it reduces memory constraints, model parallelism can be slower due to the added communication overhead between devices.

A hybrid approach often combines data and model parallelism, enabling efficient training of extremely large LLMs by distributing both data and model components across devices.

Pipeline Parallelism and Sharded Data Loading

To further optimize distributed training, pipeline parallelism and sharded data loading techniques are used:

- **Pipeline Parallelism**: Pipeline parallelism divides the model into stages, each processed in sequence across different GPUs. As one stage finishes processing, it hands off to the next, enabling overlapping computations across GPUs. This approach is beneficial for deep models with multiple layers, as it reduces idle time for each device.

- **Sharded Data Loading**: With large datasets, loading data can become a bottleneck. Sharded data loading splits the dataset across multiple nodes, allowing each to load and preprocess its own data subset. This method reduces I/O bottlenecks and improves training throughput, especially in data-heavy LLMs.

All-Reduce Operations and Communication Optimization

Efficient communication is crucial for distributed training, especially in data parallelism where gradient synchronization is required. All-Reduce operations, which aggregate and distribute gradients across nodes, are optimized with techniques like ring All-Reduce or hierarchical All-Reduce. These methods reduce the time and bandwidth required for gradient sharing, making distributed training more efficient.

Leveraging distributed training technologies such as Horovod, DeepSpeed, and TensorFlow's distributed training capabilities can make large-scale LLM training feasible and manageable. These frameworks handle much of the complexity of device management, communication, and synchronization, allowing developers to focus on model architecture and hyperparameter tuning.

Chapter: Advanced Interpretability Techniques for LLMs

Understanding how large language models make decisions is critical in applications where transparency is required, such as healthcare, finance, and law. However, the complexity of LLMs can make them difficult to interpret. Advanced interpretability techniques help developers and stakeholders understand model behavior, identify biases, and improve model reliability.

Attention Mechanisms and Visualizations

Attention mechanisms, which help LLMs focus on important parts of the input data, offer a starting point for interpretability. Visualizing attention weights can reveal how the model processes and prioritizes information within input text. Attention visualizations are particularly useful in models like Transformers, where multiple layers of attention help capture context across the entire input sequence.

Tools like BertViz and transformer visualization libraries allow users to inspect attention heads and layers, showing which parts of the input influence each decision. For example, in a medical diagnosis model, attention visualization can show which symptoms or keywords the model focused on when generating a diagnosis.

Feature Attribution and Layer-Wise Relevance Propagation

Feature attribution techniques aim to determine which input features (e.g., words or phrases) have the most significant impact on the model's output. Integrated gradients, SHAP (Shapley Additive Explanations), and LIME (Local Interpretable Model-agnostic Explanations) are common methods that assign importance scores to features, providing insight into the model's decision process.

Layer-Wise Relevance Propagation (LRP) goes further by tracing the contribution of each feature back through the layers of the model. This technique is particularly helpful for understanding complex neural networks, as it provides a granular breakdown of how each layer contributes to the final prediction. For LLMs, LRP can reveal how linguistic structures such as syntax or context influence the model's understanding of a text.

Probing Models with Auxiliary Tasks

Probing is a technique where an LLM's internal representations are examined through auxiliary tasks. Probing tasks are designed to test whether specific linguistic knowledge, such as syntax, semantics, or world knowledge, is encoded within the model's layers. By analyzing the model's performance on these tasks, researchers can understand what types of information are captured by each layer of the model.

For example, probing might involve testing whether certain model layers are responsible for tasks like sentiment analysis, entity recognition, or syntactic parsing. If specific layers show strong performance on these tasks, it suggests that the model organizes information in a structured way. This insight can help developers understand the depth and nature of the model's knowledge, which is especially important in applications requiring high accuracy and reliability.

Counterfactual Explanations and Fairness Audits

Counterfactual explanations are interpretability tools that explore how minor changes to input data would affect the model's predictions. For instance, in a hiring model, a counterfactual explanation might test whether changing a candidate's education level alters the model's recommendation. This technique helps detect biases and unintended dependencies in the model.

Fairness audits, which systematically evaluate a model's performance across different demographic groups, are another interpretability approach that addresses ethical concerns. By examining whether the model behaves differently for various groups, developers can ensure the model's decisions are fair and unbiased.

Interpretability tools like Fairness Indicators and AI Fairness 360 facilitate fairness audits, providing metrics and visualizations that help identify and mitigate potential biases.

Advanced interpretability techniques empower stakeholders to trust and understand LLMs, fostering responsible AI use in sensitive applications and improving model transparency.

Ethical Considerations (Brief Overview)

- **Bias and Fairness**: Regularly audit your models for biases and ensure fairness across different user groups.

- **Privacy**: Implement strict data privacy measures, including encryption and anonymization, to protect user data.

- **Transparency**: Make your models' decision-making processes transparent to build trust with users and stakeholders.

www.ingramcontent.com/pod-product-compliance
Lightning Source LLC
LaVergne TN
LVHW051606050326
832903LV00033B/4383